A Gift for:

_____

From:

_____

May the God of hope fill you
with all joy and peace as you trust in him,
so that you may overflow with hope
by the power of the Holy Spirit.

ROMANS 15:13

footprints

One night I dreamed a dream.
I was walking along the beach with my Lord.
Across the dark sky flashed scenes from my life.
For each scene, I noticed two sets of footprints in
   the sand,
one belonging to me
and one to my Lord.
When the last scene of my life shot before me
I looked back at the footprints in the sand
and to my surprise
I noticed that many times along the path of my life
There was only one set of footprints.
I realized that this was at the lowest
and saddest times of my life.
This always bothered me
and I questioned the Lord
about my dilemma.
"Lord, you told me when I decided to follow You,
You would walk and talk with me all the way.
But I'm aware that during the most troublesome
times of my life there is only one set of footprints.
I just don't understand why, when I needed You
   most, You leave me."
He whispered, "My precious child,
I love you and will never leave you
never, ever, during your trials and testings.
When you saw only one set of footprints
it was then that I carried you."

✝
footprints

Scripture with Reflections
Inspired by the Best-loved Poem
by Margaret Fishback Powers

Introduction

Every now and then during our devotional time, my husband, Paul, and I reread the poem I wrote for him back in 1964. During these times of renewal and prayer, we talk over the events of our lives and share burdens we have for ourselves and others. Very often, we realize that the Great Shepherd has once again reached out and carried us through the day as we spend these introspective moments together.

If the pleasure of sharing these thoughts anew has taught us anything, it is this: that God's Word is true. Our heavenly Father is faithful and will never leave us or forsake us. As we come to him daily, willing to be shaped and directed, his Word gives guideposts of clear direction. Almost everything we read, see, and experience shows us in some way that, although we do not visibly see God, he is with us. Over centuries of time, others have looked back to understand that God's Spirit and presence were there, even when they felt alone.

In our quiet moments of reflection, in the fellowship of others, and even in dreams, God opens the doors to our hearts. This is what happened when I originally wrote the poem "Footprints."

After hours of wrestling with the darkness of doubt and despair, I finally surrendered to him and, in the early-morning light of peace, wrote the poem as result of that spiritual experience.

Listen for the gentle stirring of God's grace in your own mind and soul as you read these verses of encouragement. Reflecting on his Word will help you to know him better.

Spiritual growth is not so much what we have done, but the feeling of love for him we put into everything we do. It is not so much in knowing about God that we grow, but in getting to know him in a personal, relational way. It is in becoming "a friend of God" as Abraham did that we grow in his grace, talking with him as our companion along the way, and letting God sift our thoughts and plans through the standards of his Word. May these verses encourage you anew each day as you walk with him.

MARGARET FISHBACK POWERS

God Is With Us...
In Our Dreams

One night I dreamed a dream.

Some of our dreams can have a powerful effect on us. All of us have, at one time or another, awakened laughing or fretful—and all because of a dream. The Bible tells us about many people who had dreams and visions that were given to them by God ...

[Jacob] had a dream in which he saw a stairway resting on the earth, with its top reaching to heaven, and the angels of God were ascending and descending on it.

GENESIS 28:12

Joseph had a dream, and when he told it to his brothers, they hated him all the more.

GENESIS 37:5

At Gibeon the Lord appeared to Solomon during the night in a dream, and God said, "Ask for whatever you want me to give you."

1 KINGS 3:5

An angel of the Lord appeared to Joseph in a dream. "Get up," he said, "take the child and his mother and escape to Egypt. Stay there until I tell you, for Herod is going to search for the child to kill him."

MATTHEW 2:13

After Herod died, an angel of the Lord appeared in a dream to Joseph in Egypt and said, "Get up, take the child and his mother and go to the land of Israel, for those who were trying to take the child's life are dead."

MATTHEW 2:19–20

One day at about three in the afternoon [Cornelius] had a vision. He distinctly saw an angel of God, who came to him and said, "Cornelius!"

ACTS 10:3

During the night Paul had a vision of a man of Macedonia standing and begging him, "Come over to Macedonia and help us."

ACTS 16:9

Some of our dreams are disappointing, but these are "wishful-thinking" dreams, things we come up with in our own minds, circumstances or situations that we wish would happen. Only a small portion of these kinds of dreams ever come true. In fact, these dreams can be harmful if we allow them to fill us with false hope...

This is what the Lord Almighty says:
"Do not listen to what the prophets are prophesying to you; they fill you with false hopes. They speak visions from their own minds, not from the mouth of the Lord."

JEREMIAH 23:16

Yet we should not ignore our dreams. God will sometimes use our dreams to assure us of his promises or to tell us something about himself. And when God does speak to us in dreams, he will also help us understand them...

> [God] said, "Listen to my words: "When a prophet of the Lord is among you, I reveal myself to him in visions, I speak to him in dreams."
>
> NUMBERS 12:6

> [The Lord says,] I will pour out my Spirit on all people. Your sons and daughters will prophesy, your old men will dream dreams, your young men will see visions.
>
> JOEL 2:28

God's presence with us is a reality. Acts 2:17 also tells us that God will pour his "Spirit on all people." As we dream our dreams with the knowledge that God is with us, we will begin to see things as Christ does and dream dreams inspired by the Holy Spirit that are worth re-telling and following.

God Is With Us...
In Our
Daily Walk

I was walking along the
beach with my Lord.

A close walk with the Lord is an important part of a believer's life...

[God] will teach us his ways, so that we may walk in his paths.

ISAIAH 2:3

May [God] turn our hearts to him, to walk in all his ways and to keep the commands, decrees and regulations he gave our fathers.

1 KINGS 8:58

Your love is ever before me, [Lord,] and I walk continually in your truth.

PSALM 26:3

Walk in the way of understanding.

PROVERBS 9:6

He whose walk is upright fears the Lord.

PROVERBS 14:2

The ways of the Lord are right;the righteous walk in them.

HOSEA 14:9

He whose walk is blameless is kept safe.

PROVERBS 28:18

Let us walk in the light of the Lord.

ISAIAH 2:5

Whether you turn to the right or to the left, your ears will hear a voice behind you, saying, "This is the way; walk in it."

ISAIAH 30:21

The Bible tells us that maintaining a close walk with God is a command we must obey, not merely a suggestion we may want to consider.

I am God Almighty; walk before me and be blameless.

GENESIS 17:1

What does the Lord your God ask of you but to fear the Lord your God, to walk in all his ways, to love him, to serve the Lord your God with all your heart and with all your soul.

DEUTERONOMY 10:12

Love the Lord your God...walk in all his ways... hold fast to him.

DEUTERONOMY 11:22

The Lord will establish you...if you keep the commands of the Lord your God and walk in his ways.

DEUTERONOMY 28:9

[God] has showed you, O man, what is good.
And what does the Lord require of you?
To act justly and to love mercy and to walk
humbly with your God.

MICAH 6:8

This is love: that we walk in obedience to [God's]
commands. As you have heard from the beginning,
his command is that you walk in love.

2 JOHN 6

Obey me, and I will be your God and you will be
my people. Walk in all the ways I command you,
that it may go well with you.

JEREMIAH 7:23

Be very careful to keep the commandment and
the law that Moses the servant of the Lord gave you:
to love the Lord your God, to walk in all his ways,
to obey his commands, to hold fast to him and to
serve him with all your heart and all your soul.

JOSHUA 22:5

But what does a walk with God actually entail? How does God want us to live?

> Love the Lord your God with all your heart and with all your soul and with all your strength. These commandments that I give you today are to be upon your hearts. Impress them on your children. Talk about them when you sit at home and when you walk along the road, when you lie down and when you get up.
>
> <small>DEUTERONOMY 6:5–7</small>

> He whose walk is blamelessand who does what is righteous,who speaks the truth from his heart and has no slander on his tongue, who does his neighbor no wrong and casts no slur on his fellowman, who despises a vile man but honors those who fear the Lord, who keeps his oath even when it hurts, who lends his money without usury and does not accept a bribe against the innocent. He who does these things will never be shaken.
>
> <small>PSALM 15:2–5</small>

Many of these things that God asks us to do go against our nature. Yet Nehemiah asks us, "Shouldn't you walk in the fear of our God to avoid...reproach?" (NEHEMIAH 5:9). The Bible urges us to consistently walk with the Lord, walking by faith, even when it's difficult.

Live a life worthy of the Lord...please him in every way: bearing fruit in every good work, growing in the knowledge of God.

COLOSSIANS 1:10

Just as you received Christ Jesus as Lord, continue to live in him.

COLOSSIANS 2:6

If we walk in the light, as he is in the light, we have fellowship with one another, and the blood of Jesus, his Son, purifies us from all sin.

1 JOHN 1:7

Whoever claims to live in [God] must walk as Jesus did.

1 JOHN 2:6

We live by faith, not by sight.

2 CORINTHIANS 5:7

[Jesus said,] "Walk while you have the light, before darkness overtakes you. The man who walks in the dark does not know where he is going. Put your trust in the light while you have it, so that you may become sons of light."

JOHN 12:35–36

Live a life of love, just as Christ loved us.

EPHESIANS 5:2

Health professionals suggest that people who want to become physically fit should try a consistent program of walking. Sustained walking several times a week will improve your muscle tone and strengthen your heart.

The Bible reassures us that our spiritual lives will also reap benefits when we are consistent in walking with the Lord. Look at the many benefits a walk with God provides ...

Walk in all the way that the Lord your God has commanded you, so that you may live and prosper and prolong your days in the land that you will possess.

DEUTERONOMY 5:33

I will walk among you and be your God, and you will be my people.

LEVITICUS 26:12

I command you today to love the Lord your God, to walk in his ways, and to keep his commands, decrees and laws; then you will live and increase, and the Lord your God will bless you.

DEUTERONOMY 30:16

Observe what the Lord your God requires: Walk in his ways...so that you may prosper in all you do and wherever you go.

1 KINGS 2:3

Blessed are they whose ways are blameless, who walk according to the law of the Lord. Blessed are they who keep his statutes and seek him with all their heart. They do nothing wrong; they walk in his ways.

PSALM 119:1—3

[God said,] "If you walk in my ways and obey my statutes and commands...I will give you a long life."

1 KINGS 3:14

[The Lord says,] "If you do whatever I command you and walk in my ways and do what is right in my eyes by keeping my statutes and commands... I will be with you."

1 KINGS 11:38

Blessed are all who fear the Lord, who walk
in his ways. You will eat the fruit of your labor;
blessings and prosperity will be yours.

PSALM 128:1–2

I guide you in the way of wisdom and lead you along
straight paths. When you walk, your steps will not be
hampered; when you run, you will not stumble.

PROVERBS 4:11–12

The Lord God is a sun and shield; the Lord bestows
favor and honor; no good thing does he withhold
from those whose walk is blameless.

PSALM 84:11

[The Lord says,] "Obey me, and I will be your
God and you will be my people. Walk in all the
ways I command you, that it may go well with you."

JEREMIAH 7:23

We are the temple of the living God. As God has said: "I will live with them and walk among them, and I will be their God, and they will be my people."

2 CORINTHIANS 6:16

This is what the Lord says: "Stand at the crossroads and look; ask for the ancient paths, ask where the good way is, and walk in it, and you will find rest for your souls."

JEREMIAH 6:16

Fanny Crosby once said that the Lord "lovingly guards my footsteps and gives me songs in the night." A joyful heart is the mark of one who has a consistent walk with the Lord, who follows in the footsteps of the Master.

Take strength then, and be blessed in a close walk with the Lord, for "I will strengthen them in the Lord and in his name they will walk," declares the Lord (ZECHARIAH 10:12).

God Is With Us...
In the
Hard Times

Across the dark sky
flashed scenes from my life.

We all go through times when life seems to overwhelm us. The Bible reassures us that God's presence is with us to help us, even when we don't realize it.

God is our refuge and strength, an ever-present help in trouble.

PSALM 46:1

In my distress I called to the Lord, and he answered me... I called for help, and you listened to my cry.

JONAH 2:2

Those who know your name will trust in you, for you, Lord, have never forsaken those who seek you.

PSALM 9:10

You are my hiding place; you will protect me from trouble and surround me with songs of deliverance.

PSALM 32:7

My soul finds rest in God alone; my salvation comes from him. He alone is my rock and my salvation; he is my fortress, I will never be shaken.

PSALM 62:1–2

Praise be to the Lord, to God our Savior,
who daily bears our burdens.

PSALM 68:19

Moments of darkness in our lives may be caused by the death of a loved one, the loss of a job or a home, or another great tragedy of life. Yet there is a greater darkness than these tragedies: the darkness in the eyes of one who has not felt God's love, grace, and the assurance of his hope. There is hope for all of us. There is light. Jesus Christ, the Son of God, is our hope and light in the darkness.

For you were once darkness, but now you are light in the Lord. Live as children of light.

EPHESIANS 5:8

Let him who walks in the dark, who has no light,
trust in the name of the Lord and rely on his God.

ISAIAH 50:10

The people walking in darkness have seen a great
light; on those living in the land of the shadow
of death a light has dawned.

ISAIAH 9:2

[Jesus] said, "I am the light of the world. Whoever
follows me will never walk in darkness, but will have
the light of life."

JOHN 8:12

[Jesus said,] "I have come into the world as a
light, so that no one who believes in me should
stay in darkness."

JOHN 12:46

Darkness covers the earth and thick darkness is over the peoples, but the Lord rises upon you and his glory appears over you.

ISAIAH 60:2

The Lord will be your everlasting light, and your God will be your glory.

ISAIAH 60:19

Though I have fallen, I will rise. Though I sit in darkness, the Lord will be my light... He will bring me out into the light; I will see his righteousness.

MICAH 7:8–9

Because of the tender mercy of our God...
the rising sun will come to us from heaven to shine on those living in darkness and in the shadow of death, to guide our feet into the path of peace.

LUKE 1:78–79

Our dark times may also be times when God wants to teach us something more about ourselves and his love for us. Our faith can be strengthened if we will wait patiently and trust God's heart-desire to make us more like himself.

A righteous man may have many troubles,
but the Lord delivers him from them all.

PSALM 34:19

Though you have made me see troubles, many and bitter, you will restore my life again; from the depths of the earth you will again bring me up.

PSALM 71:20

We must go through many hardships to enter the kingdom of God.

ACTS 14:22

Our light and momentary troubles are achieving for us an eternal glory that far outweighs them all. So we fix our eyes not on what is seen, but on what is unseen. For what is seen is temporary, but what is unseen is eternal.

2 CORINTHIANS 4:17–18

Be joyful in hope, patient in affliction, faithful in prayer.

ROMANS 12:12

Do not be surprised at the painful trial you are suffering, as though something strange were happening to you. But rejoice that you participate in the sufferings of Christ, so that you may be overjoyed when his glory is revealed.

1 PETER 4:12–13

Tragedy or testing, dark days or dreary nights, God knows what we are facing. He is in touch with what is happening to us, and he is concerned.

His eyes are on the ways of men; he sees their every step.

JOB 34:21

[Jesus said,] "I have told you these things, so that in me you may have peace. In this world you will have trouble. But take heart! I have overcome the world."

JOHN 16:33

Though I walk in the midst of trouble, you preserve my life... with your right hand you save me.

PSALM 138:7

He knows the way that I take; when he has tested me, I will come forth as gold.

JOB 23:10

I will be glad and rejoice in your love, for you saw my affliction and knew the anguish of my soul.

PSALM 31:7

When you pass through the waters, I will be with you; and when you pass through the rivers, they will not sweep over you. When you walk through the fire, you will not be burned; the flames will not set you ablaze.

ISAIAH 43:2

God Is With Us...
As Our
Companion

For each scene, I noticed
two sets of footprints in
the sand, one belonging to me
and one to my Lord.

I have a friend who loves to take long walks with me. We talk and laugh and enjoy each other's company as we stroll along. The exercise is beneficial, and so is the conversation.

The Lord is a lot like my friend. He enjoys walking with us as our companion on life's pathway. And he brings blessing into our lives when we walk closely with him.

If we walk in the light, as he is in the light, we have fellowship with one another, and the blood of Jesus, his Son, purifies us from all sin.

1 JOHN 1:7

Walk in [God's] ways, and keep his decrees and commands, his laws and requirements... so that you may prosper in all you do and wherever you go.

1 KINGS 2:3

Blessed are those who have learned to acclaim you, who walk in the light of your presence, O Lord.

PSALM 89:15

Walk in all the way that the Lord your God has commanded you, so that you may live and prosper and prolong your days in the land that you will possess.

DEUTERONOMY 5:33

I will walk among you and be your God, and you will be my people

LEVITICUS 26:12

"If you walk in my ways and obey my statutes and commands...I will give you a long life," [says the Lord.]

1 Kings 3:14

Blessed are all who fear the Lord, who walk in his ways. You will eat the fruit of your labor; blessings and prosperity will be yours.

Psalm 128:1–2

Come... let us walk in the light of the Lord.

Isaiah 2:5

We are the temple of the living God. As God has said: "I will live with them and walk among them, and I will be their God, and they will be my people."

2 Corinthians 6:16

[The Lord said,] "If you do whatever I command you and walk in my ways and do what is right in my eyes by keeping my statutes and commands... I will be with you."

1 Kings 11:38

Ask where the good way is, and walk in it, and you will find rest for your souls.

Jeremiah 6:16

Though I walk in the midst of trouble, you
preserve my life; you stretch out your hand...
with your right hand you save me.

PSALM 138:7

The awareness of God's presence with us is
encouraging and heartwarming. It is as if
we were two friends seated beside a rippling
brook, enjoying a gentle breeze on a warm
spring afternoon.

"Here I am! I stand at the door and knock. If
anyone hears my voice and opens the door, I will
come in and eat with him, and he with me," says
the Lord.

REVELATION 3:20

Come near to God and he will come near to you.

JAMES 4:8

"Abraham believed God, and it was credited to him
as righteousness," and he was called God's friend.

JAMES 2:23

I am a friend to all who fear you, to all who follow
your precepts.

PSALM 119:63

[Jesus said,] "You are my friends if you do what I command....I have called you friends, for everything that I learned from my Father I have made known to you. You did not choose me, but I chose you."

JOHN 15:14–16

Even when we are surrounded by family and friends, some problems seem to double in size of their own accord. If we toss and turn in the early morning hours thinking about them, they become ten times as large. Yet, although it may seem the whole world has gone wrong around us, we are not alone—God is with us!

So do not fear, for I am with you; do not be dismayed, for I am your God. I will strengthen you and help you; I will uphold you with my righteous right hand.

ISAIAH 41:10

[Jesus said,] "I will not leave you as orphans; I will come to you."

JOHN 14:18

"For where two or three come together in my name, there am I with them," [Jesus said.]

MATTHEW 18:20

Who shall separate us from the love of Christ? Shall trouble or hardship or persecution or famine or nakedness or danger or sword?... No, in all these things we are more than conquerors through him who loved us. For I am convinced that neither death nor life, neither angels nor demons, neither the present nor the future, nor any powers, neither height nor depth, nor anything else in all creation, will be able to separate us from the love of God that is in Christ Jesus our Lord.

ROMANS 8:35–39

For the Lord your God is a merciful God; he will not abandon or destroy you or forget the covenant with your forefathers, which he confirmed to them by oath.

DEUTERONOMY 4:31

God is our refuge and strength, an ever-present help in trouble.

PSALM 46:1

"Though the mountains be shaken and the hills be removed, yet my unfailing love for you will not be shaken nor my covenant of peace be removed," says the Lord, who has compassion on you.

ISAIAH 54:10

"He will call upon me, and I will answer him;
I will be with him in trouble, I will deliver him
and honor him. With long life will I satisfy him
and show him my salvation," [says the Lord.]

PSALM 91:15–16

[Lord,] where can I go from your Spirit? Where
can I flee from your presence? If I go up to the
heavens, you are there; if I make my bed in the
depths, you are there. If I rise on the wings of
the dawn, if I settle on the far side of the sea, even
there your hand will guide me, your right hand
will hold me fast.

PSALM 139:7–10

Wherever we go, we cannot step outside the boundaries of God's love and care. We can have fellowship "with the Father and with his Son, Jesus Christ" wherever we are (1 JOHN 1:3). All we need to do is trust in God's loving companionship and walk the path he has placed before us.

> He will not let your foot slip — he who watches over you will not slumber. The Lord watches over you— the Lord is your shade at your right hand; the sun will not harm you by day, nor the moon by night. The Lord will keep you from all harm — he will watch over your life; the Lord will watch over your coming and going both now and forevermore.
>
> PSALM 121:3, 5—8

> [Then Jesus said,] "And surely I am with you always, to the very end of the age."
>
> MATTHEW 28:20

God Is With Us...
Never Look Back!
No Regrets!

When the last scene of my life
shot before me, I looked back
at the footprints in the sand.

We say that hindsight is always 20/20. Looking back is something we often do without considering the consequences. However, looking back is not recommended in the Bible. Lot was warned not to look back toward Sodom and Gomorrah...

> With the coming of dawn, the angels urged Lot, saying..."Flee for your lives! Don't look back, and don't stop anywhere in the plain! Flee to the mountains or you will be swept away!" Then the Lord rained down burning sulfur on Sodom and Gomorrah. ..Thus he overthrew those cities and the entire plain... But Lot's wife looked back, and she became a pillar of salt.
>
> GENESIS 19:15, 17, 24–26

Joshua and his men attacked their enemies in the city of Ai and quickly set the city on fire. When the men of Ai looked back, disaster fell on them...

> The men of Ai looked back and saw the smoke of the city rising against the sky, but they had no chance to escape in any direction, for the Israelites who had been fleeing toward the desert had turned back against their pursuers.
>
> JOSHUA 8:20

Even the Lord Jesus reminded his listeners of the perils of looking back...

> Jesus replied, "No one who puts his hand to the plow and looks back is fit for service in the kingdom of God."
>
> LUKE 9:62

When we live with an attitude that looks back over our lives with "if onlys" and regrets, we rob ourselves of hope. We rob ourselves of the joy of God's grace.

> ["God] has delivered us from such a deadly peril, and he will deliver us. On him we have set our hope that he will continue to deliver us."
>
> 2 CORINTHIANS 1:10

> I do not consider myself yet to have taken hold of it. But one thing I do: Forgetting what is behind and straining toward what is ahead, I press on toward the goal to win the prize for which God has called me heavenward in Christ Jesus.
>
> PHILIPPIANS 3:13—14

God never changes. He is the God of grace. He is the God of hope. He is the God of love who offers us a life free of regrets.

> God is greater than our hearts, and he knows everything.
>
> 1 JOHN 3:20

> From everlasting to everlasting the Lord's love is with those who fear him, and his righteousness with their children's children— with those who keep his covenant and remember to obey his precepts.
>
> PSALM 103:17–18

A life without regrets does not mean a life without repentance. When we sin, we must go beyond regretting and feeling sorry for our actions. We must move on to repentance by turning from our sinful ways and embracing God's forgiveness.

> Godly sorrow brings repentance that leads to salvation and leaves no regret.
>
> 2 CORINTHIANS 7:10

Cleanse me with hyssop, and I will be clean;
wash me, and I will be whiter than snow....
Hide your face from my sins and blot out all my
iniquity. Create in me a pure heart, O God, and
renew a steadfast spirit within me. Do not cast me
from your presence or take your Holy Spirit from
me. Restore to me the joy of your salvation and
grant me a willing spirit, to sustain me.

PSALM 51:7–12

When we have experienced God's forgiveness,
we are new creatures. We do not need to live
a life of regrets, but rather we can live with a
forward-looking hope of glory!

Let us throw off everything that hinders and the sin
that so easily entangles, and let us run with perseverance the race marked out for us. Let us fix our
eyes on Jesus, the author and perfecter of our faith.

HEBREWS 12:1–2

If anyone is in Christ, he is a new creation; the old
has gone, the new has come!

2 CORINTHIANS 5:17

I have fought the good fight, I have finished the
race, I have kept the faith. Now there is in store
for me the crown of righteousness, which the Lord,
the righteous Judge, will award to me on that day.

2 TIMOTHY 4:7–8

Whenever we do look back over our lives,
we must do so with God's perspective—no re-
morse or regrets. With God's perspective, we
will be able to trace his hand on our lives and
see that he has swept up the bad things of life
and transformed them into good, just as he
promised he would. With God's perspective,
we will be able to live above regrets and live
in God's peace and joy.

We know that in all things God works for the
good of those who love him, who have been called
according to his purpose.

ROMANS 8:28

Surely goodness and love will follow me all
the days of my life, and I will dwell in the house
of the Lord forever.

PSALM 23:6

God Is With Us...
In Our Loneliness

There was only one set of footprints.

Toddlers often face separation anxiety—a feeling of abandonment whenever their parents leave the room. Though we may be much older and wiser than little children, we still feel the pain of loneliness and isolation. Both Jesus and the psalmist also knew what it was to feel alone, abandoned, forgotten ...

About the ninth hour Jesus cried out in a loud voice, "Eloi, Eloi, lama sabachthani?"—which means, "My God, my God, why have you forsaken me?"

MATTHEW 27:46

Do not hide your face from me, do not turn your servant away in anger; you have been my helper. Do not reject me or forsake me, O God my Savior.

PSALM 27:9

I say to God my Rock, "Why have you forgotten me? Why must I go about mourning, oppressed by the enemy?"

PSALM 42:9

When we feel alone and abandoned we can take comfort in God's promises to deliver us from our isolation and pain.

Can a mother forget the baby at her breast and have no compassion on the child she has borne? Though she may forget, I will not forget you! See, I have engraved you on the palms of my hands.

ISAIAH 49:15–16

I the Lord will answer them; I, the God of Israel, will not forsake them.

ISAIAH 41:17

You are enthroned as the Holy One; you are the praise of Israel. In you our fathers put their trust; they trusted and you delivered them. They cried to you and were saved; in you they trusted and were not disappointed.

PSALM 22:3–5

The Lord will not reject his people, because
the Lord was pleased to make you his own.

1 SAMUEL 12:22

[Jesus said,] "I will not leave you as orphans;
I will come to you."

JOHN 14:18

God is our refuge and strength, an ever-present
help in trouble.

PSALM 46:1

The eternal God is your refuge, and underneath
are the everlasting arms.

DEUTERONOMY 33:27

"Though the mountains be shaken and the hills
be removed, yet my unfailing love for you will not
be shaken nor my covenant of peace be removed,"
says the Lord.

ISAIAH 54:10

"Do not let your hearts be troubled. Trust in God;
trust also in me," [Jesus said.]

JOHN 14:1

How great is your goodness, [O Lord,] which you have stored up for those who fear you, which you bestow in the sight of men on those who take refuge in you. In the shelter of your presence you hide them... in your dwelling you keep them safe.

PSALM 31:19–20

He will not let your foot slip— he who watches over you will not slumber. The Lord watches over you— the Lord is your shade at your right hand; the sun will not harm you by day, nor the moon by night. The Lord will keep you from all harm—he will watch over your life; the Lord will watch over your coming and going both now and forevermore.

PSALM 121:3, 5–8

God is always with us—in our joy and in our pain, in the good times and in the bad times. His steadfast love and faithfulness are promises to which we can cling, promises to bring us joy when we face loneliness.

[And Jesus told his disciples,] "And surely I am with you always, to the very end of the age."

MATTHEW 28:20

The Lord your God is a merciful God; he will not abandon or destroy you.

DEUTERONOMY 4:31

Be strong and courageous. Do not be afraid or terrified...for the Lord your God goes with you; he will never leave you nor forsake you.

DEUTERONOMY 31:6

"Here I am! I stand at the door and knock. If anyone hears my voice and opens the door, I will come in and eat with him, and he with me," [says the Lord.]

REVELATION 3:20

You have made him glad with the joy of your presence.

PSALM 21:6

Those who know your name will trust in you, for you, Lord, have never forsaken those who seek you.

PSALM 9:10

[O Lord,] Where can I go from your Spirit?
Where can I flee from your presence? If I go up
to the heavens, you are there; if I make my bed in
the depths, you are there. If I rise on the wings of
the dawn, if I settle on the far side of the sea, even
there your hand will guide me, your right hand
will hold me fast.

PSALM 139:7—10

When loneliness overtakes us, we need to
remember that we are not alone. God has
promised to be with us. He will never forsake
us. Lean on his promises and receive his peace.

Why are you downcast, O my soul? Why
so disturbed within me? Put your hope in
God, for I will yet praise him, my Savior
and my God.

PSALM 42:11

"I will be with you; I will never leave you nor
forsake you," [says the Lord.]

JOSHUA 1:5

Who shall separate us from the love of Christ?
Shall trouble or hardship or persecution or famine
or nakedness or danger or sword?... No, in all
these things we are more than conquerors through
him who loved us. For I am convinced that neither
death nor life, neither angels nor demons, neither
the present nor the future, nor any powers, neither
height nor depth, nor anything else in all creation,
will be able to separate us from the love of God that
is in Christ Jesus our Lord.

ROMANS 8:35–39

God Is With Us...
In Our Sorrow

I realized that this was at the
lowest and saddest times of my life.

Sorrow can cause us to doubt God's plan. The psalmist cried, "Has his unfailing love vanished forever? Has his promise failed for all time? Has God forgotten to be merciful? Has he in anger withheld his compassion?" (PSALM 77:8–9). Though we may face trouble and difficulties, sadness and pain, God is still in control, and he is always with us.

When I said, "My foot is slipping," your love, O Lord, supported me. When anxiety was great within me, your consolation brought joy to my soul.

PSALM 94:18–19

The Lord upholds all those who fall and lifts up all who are bowed down.

PSALM 145:14

The Lord is a refuge for the oppressed, a stronghold in times of trouble.

PSALM 9:9

The eternal God is your refuge, and underneath
are the everlasting arms.

DEUTERONOMY 33:27

We must remember to listen closely to God's
voice when trouble rages around us. When the
agonies of life begin to crush us, God has not
moved away from us. Often we have moved
away from him. We need to return to him
in faith and call on him for his strength.

I have put my trust in you. Show me the way
I should go, for to you I lift up my soul.

PSALM 143:8

The Lord...makes his steps firm; though he
stumble, he will not fall, for the Lord upholds
him with his hand.

PSALM 37:23–24

I sought the Lord, and he answered me; he
delivered me from all my fears.

PSALM 34:4

A righteous man may have many troubles,
but the Lord delivers him from them all.

PSALM 34:19

My soul finds rest in God alone; my salvation
comes from him. He alone is my rock and my
salvation; he is my fortress, I will never be shaken.

PSALM 62:1–2

Do not let your hearts be troubled. Trust in God.

JOHN 14:1

[Jesus said,] "Peace I leave with you; my peace I give
you. I do not give to you as the world gives. Do not
let your hearts be troubled and do not be afraid."

JOHN 14:27

[Jesus told his disciples,] "In this world you will have
trouble. But take heart! I have overcome the world."

JOHN 16:33

[Jesus] said to me, "My grace is sufficient for you,
for my power is made perfect in weakness."

2 CORINTHIANS 12:9

Praise be to the God and Father of our Lord Jesus Christ, the Father of compassion and the God of all comfort, who comforts us in all our troubles, so that we can comfort those in any trouble with the comfort we ourselves have received from God.

2 Corinthians 1:3–4

The Lord has anointed me... to comfort all who mourn... and...to bestow on them a crown of beauty instead of ashes, the oil of gladness instead of mourning, and a garment of praise instead of a spirit of despair.

Isaiah 61:1–3

My comfort in my suffering is this: Your promise preserves my life, [O Lord.]

Psalm 119:50

We do not have a high priest who is unable to sympathize with our weaknesses....Let us then approach the throne of grace with confidence, so that we may receive mercy and find grace to help us in our time of need.

Hebrews 4:15–16

Jesus experienced sorrow of the deepest kind in the Garden of Gethsemane—the sorrow of impending death. We also experience pain when death takes a loved one, but God reminds us that he is still in control. Death is not the master—God is.

> For none of us lives to himself alone and none of us dies to himself alone. If we live, we live to the Lord; and if we die, we die to the Lord. So, whether we live or die, we belong to the Lord.
>
> ROMANS 14:7–8

> If only for this life we have hope in Christ, we are to be pitied more than all men. But Christ has indeed been raised from the dead… Since death came through a man, the resurrection of the dead comes also through a man. For as in Adam all die, so in Christ all will be made alive.
>
> 1 CORINTHIANS 15:19–22

> Listen, I tell you a mystery: We will not all sleep, but we will all be changed—in a flash, in the twinkling of an eye, at the last trumpet. For the trumpet will sound, the dead will be raised imperishable, and we will be changed.
>
> 1 CORINTHIANS 15:51–52

Even though I walk through the valley of the shadow of death, I will fear no evil, for you are with me; your rod and your staff, they comfort me.

PSALM 23:4

We believe that...God will bring with Jesus those who have fallen asleep in him...For the Lord himself will come down from heaven, with a loud command, with the voice of the archangel and with the trumpet call of God, and the dead in Christ will rise first. After that, we who are still alive and are left will be caught up together with them in the clouds to meet the Lord in the air. And so we will be with the Lord forever.

1 THESSALONIANS 4:14,16–17

For to me, to live is Christ and to die is gain.

PHILIPPIANS 1:21

Whether we face death, discouragement, loss, or pain, we can take great comfort in knowing that no sorrow is too deep that God cannot feel it with us. And God wants to help deliver us from it. He wants to bring us his divine comfort.

This I call to mind and therefore I have hope: Because of the Lord's great love we are not consumed, for his compassions never fail. They are new every morning; great is your faithfulness.

LAMENTATIONS 3:21–23

The Lord is good to those whose hope is in him, to the one who seeks him.

LAMENTATIONS 3:25

Do not be anxious about anything, but in everything, by prayer and petition, with thanksgiving, present your requests to God. And the peace of God, which transcends all understanding, will guard your hearts and your minds in Christ Jesus.

PHILIPPIANS 4:6–7

Be strong and take heart, all you who hope in the Lord.

PSALM 31:24

[God] will show compassion, so great is his
unfailing love.

LAMENTATIONS 3:32

[Jesus said,] "Come to me, all you who are weary
and burdened, and I will give you rest. Take my
yoke upon you and learn from me, for I am gentle
and humble in heart, and you will find rest for
your souls."

MATTHEW 11:28–29

"I will refresh the weary and satisfy the faint,"
[says the Lord.]

JEREMIAH 31:25

For I am the Lord, your God, who takes hold
of your right hand and says to you, Do not fear;
I will help you.

ISAIAH 41:13

In all their distress [the Lord] too was distressed,
and the angel of his presence saved them. In his
love and mercy he redeemed them; he lifted them
up and carried them.

ISAIAH 63:9

Shout for joy, O heavens; rejoice, O earth;
burst into song, O mountains! For the Lord
comforts his people and will have compassion
on his afflicted ones.

ISAIAH 49:13

I will build them up and not tear them down; I will
plant them and not uproot them. I will give them a
heart to know me, that I am the Lord. They will be
my people, and I will be their God.

JEREMIAH 24:6–7

Though things may seem hopeless, "God,
who has called you into fellowship with
his Son Jesus Christ our Lord, is faithful"
(1 CORINTHIANS 1:9). No trial is so great that God
cannot deliver us. No pain is so great that he
does not bring us comfort. And no situation
is ever without God's presence: "Do not fear,
for I am with you; do not be dismayed, for I
am your God. I will strengthen you and help
you; I will uphold you with my righteous right
hand" (ISAIAH 41:10).

God Is With Us...
Should We Fret?

This always bothered me...

Fretting and a kitchen blender have a lot in common. With the push of a button, the contents of a blender are whirled and swirled until they become a frothy mixture. In our lives, fretting gnaws away at us until our lives become a churned jumble. But God doesn't want us to live "blender-ized" lives.

> Do not fret because of evil men or be envious of those who do wrong; for like the grass they will soon wither, like green plants they will soon die away. Trust in the Lord and do good.
>
> PSALM 37:1–3

Fretting easily leads to worry; worry casts a big shadow over small problems—a shadow that should never cross our lives.

> Cast all your anxiety on [God] because he cares for you.
>
> 1 PETER 5:7

> Jesus said…"Do not worry about your life, what you will eat; or about your body, what you will wear. Life is more than food, and the body more than clothes."
>
> LUKE 12:22–23

Who of you by worrying can add a single hour to his life? And why do you worry about clothes? See how the lilies of the field grow. They do not labor or spin. Yet I tell you that not even Solomon in all his splendor was dressed like one of these. If that is how God clothes the grass of the field, which is here today and tomorrow is thrown into the fire, will he not much more clothe you, O you of little faith?

MATTHEW 6:27–30

When the outlook is not good, we should not fret. We need a change of perspective to realize that God sees tomorrow more clearly than we see yesterday. The future is completely in his hands!

When they heard that the Lord was concerned about them and had seen their misery, they bowed down and worshiped.

EXODUS 4:31

"I am concerned for you and will look on you with favor," [says the Lord.]

EZEKIEL 36:9

Don't fret! Cheer up! Neither the sun, nor the Son, have gone out of business. He is with us. A new day will dawn, and the Lord will bring himself to the center of our problems.

Blessed is the man who trusts in the Lord, whose confidence is in him. He will be like a tree planted by the water that sends out its roots by the stream. It does not fear when heat comes; its leaves are always green. It has no worries in a year of drought and never fails to bear fruit.

JEREMIAH 17:7–8

Cast your cares on the Lord and he will sustain you; he will never let the righteous fall.

PSALM 55:22

Let us then approach the throne of grace with confidence, so that we may receive mercy and find grace to help us in our time of need.

HEBREWS 4:16

The Lord is with you when you are with him. If you seek him, he will be found by you.

2 CHRONICLES 15:2

My flesh and my heart may fail, but God is the
strength of my heart and my portion forever.

PSALM 73:26

Be on your guard; stand firm in the faith; be men
of courage; be strong.

1 CORINTHIANS 16:13

He who fears the Lord has a secure fortress.

PROVERBS 14:26

Great peace have they who love [God's] law, and
nothing can make them stumble.

PSALM 119:165

God has said, "Never will I leave you; never will I
forsake you." So we say with confidence, "The Lord
is my helper; I will not be afraid. What can man do
to me?"

HEBREWS 13:5–6

The Lord himself goes before you and will be with
you; he will never leave you nor forsake you. Do
not be afraid; do not be discouraged.

DEUTERONOMY 31:8

Remember, fretting will only tie us in knots. Prayer is the only way to cut short our fretting—to untie those knots of worry and care and grant us God's peace, instead.

> Do not be anxious about anything, but in everything, by prayer and petition, with thanksgiving, present your requests to God. And the peace of God, which transcends all understanding, will guard your hearts and your minds in Christ Jesus.
>
> PHILIPPIANS 4:6–7

God Is With Us...
When We Need Direction

And I questioned the Lord
about my dilemma.

When a transit strike brought our recently purchased business to a standstill, I found myself wondering if we had made the right decision to get into this new business. The choice had seemed to be the right one at the time, but then, I wasn't so sure. How was I supposed to sort out what we should do next? When we face questions of this kind, we need to get our arms around God's wisdom ...

> If any of you lacks wisdom, he should ask God, who gives generously to all without finding fault, and it will be given to him.
>
> JAMES 1:5

> "I will instruct you and teach you in the way you should go; I will counsel you and watch over you," [says the Lord.]
>
> PSALM 32:8

> Trust in the Lord with all your heart and lean not on your own understanding; in all your ways acknowledge him, and he will make your paths straight.
>
> PROVERBS 3:5–6

For the Lord gives wisdom, and from his mouth come knowledge and understanding.

PROVERBS 2:6

Whether you turn to the right or to the left, your ears will hear a voice behind you, saying, "This is the way; walk in it."

ISAIAH 30:21

But when he, the Spirit of truth, comes, he will guide you into all truth. He will not speak on his own; he will speak only what he hears, and he will tell you what is yet to come.

JOHN 16:13

Show me your ways, O Lord, teach me your paths; guide me in your truth and teach me, for you are God my Savior, and my hope is in you all day long.

PSALM 25:4–5

This is what the Lord says— your Redeemer, the Holy One of Israel: "I am the Lord your God, who teaches you what is best for you, who directs you in the way you should go."

ISAIAH 48:17

God doesn't mind our questions when we come to him with a seeking heart. God is bigger than any question we can ask. And he often will give us the answers we seek in his Word.

Your word is a lamp to my feet and a light for my path.

PSALM 119:105

These commands are a lamp, this teaching is a light, and the corrections of discipline are the way to life.

PROVERBS 6:23

Do not let this Book of the Law depart from your mouth; meditate on it day and night, so that you may be careful to do everything written in it. Then you will be prosperous and successful.

JOSHUA 1:8

Pay attention and listen to the sayings of the wise... for it is pleasing when you keep them in your heart and have all of them ready on your lips. So that your trust may be in the Lord.

PROVERBS 22:17–19

When we find ourselves questioning God's reason for allowing certain things to happen, we must stop, remember God's faithfulness, and depend upon his grace. Whatever our questions, whatever our circumstances, God is still in control.

> If the Lord delights in a man's way, he makes his steps firm; though he stumble, he will not fall, for the Lord upholds him with his hand.
>
> PSALM 37:23–24

> Since you are my rock and my fortress, for the sake of your name lead and guide me, [O Lord.]
>
> PSALM 31:3

> And we know that in all things God works for the good of those who love him, who have been called according to his purpose.
>
> ROMANS 8:28

> The Lord will fulfill his purpose for me; your love, O Lord, endures forever— do not abandon the works of your hands.
>
> PSALM 138:8

Let us acknowledge the Lord; let us press on to acknowledge him. As surely as the sun rises, he will appear; he will come to us like the winter rains, like the spring rains that water the earth.

HOSEA 6:3

For this God is our God for ever and ever;
he will be our guide even to the end.

PSALM 48:14

When we need direction, we must trust that the Lord will take our faith, limited as it is, and make something of lasting value out of it. God has a plan for us. He cares about our dilemmas, hears our heartfelt cries, and will answer us in ways that will astonish us and fill our hearts with songs of joy.

"For I know the plans I have for you," declares the Lord, "plans to prosper you and not to harm you, plans to give you hope and a future."

JEREMIAH 29:11

God Is With Us...
In Our
Decisions

"Lord, You told me when I
decided to follow You..."

It seems that sometimes all we do is make decisions. Purchases at the grocery store are easy, but life-changing decisions are more difficult. How can God help us?

[The Lord says,] "I guide you in the way of wisdom and lead you along straight paths."

PROVERBS 4:11

The Lord gives wisdom, and from his mouth come knowledge and understanding.

PROVERBS 2:6

Do you not know? Have you not heard? The Lord is the everlasting God, the Creator of the ends of the earth. He will not grow tired or weary, and his understanding no one can fathom. He gives strength to the weary and increases the power of the weak.

ISAIAH 40:28—29

Where then does wisdom come from? Where does understanding dwell? It is hidden from the eyes of every living thing, concealed even from the birds of the air... God understands the way to it and he alone knows where it dwells.

JOB 28:20–21, 23

If any of you lacks wisdom, he should ask God, who gives generously to all without finding fault, and it will be given to him.

JAMES 1:5

The decisions we need to make may be simple or they may be complex, but they should always be predicated on our decision to follow the Lord.

What does the Lord your God ask of you but to fear the Lord your God, to walk in all his ways, to love him, to serve the Lord your God with all your heart and with all your soul, and to observe the Lord's commands and decrees that I am giving you today for your own good?

DEUTERONOMY 10:12–13

Fear the Lord and serve him faithfully with all your heart; consider what great things he has done for you.

1 SAMUEL 12:24

[Jesus said,] "Whoever acknowledges me before men, I will also acknowledge him before my Father in heaven."

MATTHEW 10:32

[Joshua said,] "Choose for yourselves this day whom you will serve...As for me and my household, we will serve the Lord."

JOSHUA 24:15

Love the Lord your God, to walk in all his ways, to obey his commands, to hold fast to him and to serve him with all your heart and all your soul.

JOSHUA 22:5

It is the Lord your God you must follow, and him you must revere. Keep his commands and obey him; serve him and hold fast to him.

DEUTERONOMY 13:4

When we decide to follow the Lord, it means we must live our lives the way he wants us to, following his commands, yielding to his control.

Those who live according to the sinful nature have their minds set on what that nature desires; but those who live in accordance with the Spirit have their minds set on what the Spirit desires.

ROMANS 8:5

The one who sows to please his sinful nature, from that nature will reap destruction; the one who sows to please the Spirit, from the Spirit will reap eternal life.

GALATIANS 6:8

Forgetting what is behind and straining toward what is ahead, I press on toward the goal to win the prize for which God has called me heavenward in Christ Jesus.

PHILIPPIANS 3:13—14

The grace of God that brings salvation has appeared to all men. It teaches us to say "No" to ungodliness and worldly passions, and to live self-controlled, upright and godly lives in this present age.

TITUS 2:11–12

Make every effort to live in peace with all men and to be holy.

HEBREWS 12:14

Offer your bodies as living sacrifices, holy and pleasing to God—this is your spiritual act of worship. Do not conform any longer to the pattern of this world, but be transformed by the renewing of your mind.

ROMANS 12:1–2

God did not call us to be impure, but to live a holy life.

1 THESSALONIANS 4:7

What does the Lord your God ask of you but to fear the Lord your God, to walk in all his ways, to love him, to serve the Lord your God with all your heart and with all your soul?

DEUTERONOMY 10:12

Pursue righteousness, godliness, faith, love, endurance and gentleness. Fight the good fight of the faith.

1 TIMOTHY 6:11–12

Serve him with wholehearted devotion and with a willing mind, for the Lord searches every heart and understands every motive behind the thoughts.

1 Chronicles 28:9

"Obey me, and I will be your God and you will be my people. Walk in all the ways I command you, that it may go well with you," [says the Lord Almighty.]

Jeremiah 7:23

Now that you have been set free from sin and have become slaves to God, the benefit you reap leads to holiness, and the result is eternal life.

Romans 6:22

Let us purify ourselves from everything that contaminates body and spirit, perfecting holiness out of reverence for God.

2 Corinthians 7:1

Be holy in all you do; for it is written: "Be holy, because I am holy."

1 Peter 1:15–16

Just as you received Christ Jesus as Lord, continue to live in him, rooted and built up in him, strengthened in the faith as you were taught, and overflowing with thankfulness.

Colossians 2:6–7

Do not turn away from the Lord, but serve the Lord with all your heart.

1 SAMUEL 12:20

Let your eyes look straight ahead, fix your gaze directly before you. Make level paths for your feet and take only ways that are firm.

PROVERBS 4:25–26

We must pay more careful attention, therefore, to what we have heard, so that we do not drift away.

HEBREWS 2:1

Let us hold unswervingly to the hope we profess, for he who promised is faithful.

HEBREWS 10:23

Since we are surrounded by such a great cloud of witnesses, let us throw off everything that hinders and the sin that so easily entangles, and let us run with perseverance the race marked out for us.

HEBREWS 12:1

This is how we know who the children of God are and who the children of the devil are: Anyone who does not do what is right is not a child of God; nor is anyone who does not love his brother.

1 JOHN 3:10

He follows my decrees and faithfully keeps my laws. That man is righteous; he will surely live, declares the Sovereign Lord.

EZEKIEL 18:9

He has showed you, O man, what is good. And what does the Lord require of you? To act justly and to love mercy and to walk humbly with your God.

MICAH 6:8

Lord, who may dwell in your sanctuary? Who may live on your holy hill? He whose walk is blameless and who does what is righteous, who speaks the truth from his heart.

PSALM 15:1–2

We all need God's divine power from day to day to follow in his footsteps—to learn the eternal, upside-down, inside-out values of God's kingdom so that we may make decisions based on his character and ultimately share in his glory.

> If anyone speaks, he should do it as one speaking the very words of God. If anyone serves, he should do it with the strength God provides, so that in all things God may be praised through Jesus Christ.
>
> 1 PETER 4:11

God Is With Us...
As Our Guide

"...You would walk and talk
with me all the way."

I saw two children walking together today, happily exchanging words and glances, laughing aloud at shared jokes. They didn't worry about the cracks in the sidewalk or the bumps in the road but, rather, skipped along over them. God wants our walk with him to be just like that—enjoying his company, sharing together, and crossing the rough places on our journey home without the slightest care.

> If we claim to have fellowship with him yet walk in the darkness, we lie and do not live by the truth. But if we walk in the light, as he is in the light, we have fellowship with one another, and the blood of Jesus, his Son, purifies us from all sin.
>
> 1 JOHN 1:6–7

> Whoever claims to live in him must walk as Jesus did.
>
> 1 JOHN 2:6

> Righteousness goes before him and prepares the way for his steps.
>
> PSALM 85:13

> O Lord...I have walked before you faithfully and with wholehearted devotion and have done what is good in your eyes.
>
> 2 KINGS 20:3

You have delivered me from death and my feet from stumbling, that I may walk before God in the light of life.

PSALM 56:13

Blessed are those who have learned to acclaim you, who walk in the light of your presence, O Lord.

PSALM 89:15

The ways of the Lord are right; the righteous walk in them, but the rebellious stumble in them.

HOSEA 14:9

Many times along our life-walk, the path becomes obscure. We need someone to help show us the way. That someone is God.

The Lord will guide you always; he will satisfy your needs in a sun-scorched land and will strengthen your frame. You will be like a well-watered garden, like a spring whose waters never fail.

ISAIAH 58:11

[God] guides me in paths of righteousness for his name's sake. Even though I walk through the valley of the shadow of death, I will fear no evil, for you are with me; your rod and your staff, they comfort me.

PSALM 23:3–4

This is what the Lord says— your Redeemer, the Holy One of Israel: "I am the Lord your God, who teaches you what is best for you, who directs you in the way you should go."

ISAIAH 48:17

[O Lord,] you guide me with your counsel.

PSALM 73:24

When he, the Spirit of truth, comes, he will guide you into all truth.

JOHN 16:13

[O Lord,] since you are my rock and my fortress, for the sake of your name lead and guide me.

PSALM 31:3

If any of you lacks wisdom, he should ask God, who gives generously to all without finding fault, and it will be given to him.

JAMES 1:5

Teach me your way, O Lord; lead me in a straight path.

PSALM 27:11

Trust in the Lord with all your heart and lean not on your own understanding; in all your ways acknowledge him, and he will make your paths straight.

PROVERBS 3:5—6

Lead me, O Lord, in your righteousness... make straight your way before me.

PSALM 5:8

Show me the way I should go, for to you I lift up my soul.

PSALM 143:8

Teach me to do your will, for you are my God; may your good Spirit lead me on level ground.

PSALM 143:10

God's Word becomes the road map for our daily walk with the Savior.

> Your word is a lamp to my feet and a light for my path, O Lord.
>
> <small>PSALM 119:105</small>

> These commands are a lamp, this teaching is a light, and the corrections of discipline are the way to life.
>
> <small>PROVERBS 6:23</small>

His Word reminds us of his power, his provision, and his sovereignty.

> Commit to the Lord whatever you do, and your plans will succeed.
>
> <small>PROVERBS 16:3</small>

> My flesh and my heart may fail, but God is the strength of my heart and my portion forever.
>
> <small>PSALM 73:26</small>

If the Lord delights in a man's way, he makes his
steps firm; though he stumble, he will not fall,
for the Lord upholds him with his hand.

PSALM 37:23–24

His Word reminds us of his love.

This I call to mind and therefore I have hope:
Because of the Lord's great love we are not consumed, for his compassions never fail. They are
new every morning; great is your faithfulness.

LAMENTATIONS 3:21–23

The Lord will fulfill [his purpose] for me;
your love, O Lord, endures forever.

PSALM 138:8

How great is the love the Father has lavished
on us, that we should be called children of God!

1 JOHN 3:1

Let's enjoy the time with God as he walks and talks with us each day, wherever we are, for "this God is our God for ever and ever; he will be our guide even to the end" (PSALM 48:14).

> "Be still, and know that I am God; I will be exalted among the nations, I will be exalted in the earth." The Lord Almighty is with us; the God of Jacob is our fortress.
>
> PSALM 46:10–11

God Is With Us...
In Our
Difficulties

But I'm aware that during the most
troublesome times of my life,
there is only one set of footprints.

Ruts and potholes. Shadows and deep darkness. The journey of life can sometimes be very troubling. We stumble and have difficulty following in God's footsteps. We are fearful of the unknown. But God's Word reminds us to trust, to believe, to hope.

> Blessed is he whose help is the God of Jacob, whose hope is in the Lord his God, the Maker of heaven and earth, the sea, and everything in them— the Lord, who remains faithful forever.
>
> PSALM 146:5–6

> Why are you downcast, O my soul? Why so disturbed within me? Put your hope in God, for I will yet praise him, my Savior and my God.
>
> PSALM 43:5–6

> You have been my hope, O Sovereign Lord, my confidence since my youth.
>
> PSALM 71:5

Blessed is the man who trusts in the Lord, whose confidence is in him.

JEREMIAH 17:7

The Lord is good to those whose hope is in him, to the one who seeks him.

LAMENTATIONS 3:25

When I am afraid, I will trust in you. In God, whose word I praise, in God I trust; I will not be afraid. What can mortal man do to me?

PSALM 56:3–4

As for me, I watch in hope for the Lord, I wait for God my Savior; my God will hear me.

MICAH 7:7

We all go through troubling times, but we must never doubt God's presence with us.

God has said, "Never will I leave you; never will I forsake you." So we say with confidence, "The Lord is my helper; I will not be afraid. What can man do to me?"

HEBREWS 13:5–6

[Jesus said,] "Surely I am with you always, to the very end of the age."

MATTHEW 28:20

Do not fear, for I am with you; do not be dismayed, for I am your God. I will strengthen you and help you; I will uphold you with my righteous right hand.

ISAIAH 41:10

The Lord your God is a merciful God; he will not abandon or destroy you.

DEUTERONOMY 4:31

Those who know your name will trust in you, for you, Lord, have never forsaken those who seek you.

PSALM 9:10

"For I know the plans I have for you," declares the Lord, "plans to prosper you and not to harm you, plans to give you hope and a future."

JEREMIAH 29:11

God will never let us down. He promises us his strength, his peace, his comfort, and his presence. All we need to do is depend on him, for we can never break God's promises by leaning on them.

Do not be afraid. Stand firm and you will see the deliverance the Lord will bring you today....The Lord will fight for you; you need only to be still.

EXODUS 14:13–14

The eternal God is your refuge, and underneath are the everlasting arms.

DEUTERONOMY 33:27

"I will build them up and not tear them down; I will plant them and not uproot them. I will give them a heart to know me, that I am the Lord. They will be my people, and I will be their God, for they will return to me with all their heart," [says the Lord.]

JEREMIAH 24:6–7

The Lord longs to be gracious to you; he rises to show you compassion.

ISAIAH 30:18

[Jesus replied,] "In this world you will have trouble. But take heart! I have overcome the world."

JOHN 16:33

We know that in all things God works for the good of those who love him, who have been called according to his purpose.

ROMANS 8:28

If the Lord delights in a man's way, he makes his steps firm; though he stumble, he will not fall, for the Lord upholds him with his hand.

PSALM 37:23—24

"Call upon me in the day of trouble; I will deliver you, and you will honor me," [says the Lord.]

PSALM 50:15

Cast your cares on the Lord and he will sustain you; he will never let the righteous fall.

PSALM 55:22

He gives strength to the weary and increases the power of the weak. Even youths grow tired and weary, and young men stumble and fall; but those who hope in the Lord will renew their strength. They will soar on wings like eagles; they will run and not grow weary, they will walk and not be faint.

ISAIAH 40:29–31

"When you pass through the waters, I will be with you; and when you pass through the rivers, they will not sweep over you. When you walk through the fire, you will not be burned; the flames will not set you ablaze," [says the Lord.]

ISAIAH 43:2

The Lord is good, a refuge in times of trouble. He cares for those who trust in him.

NAHUM 1:7

Who shall separate us from the love of Christ?
Shall trouble or hardship or persecution or famine
or nakedness or danger or sword....No, in all these
things we are more than conquerors through him
who loved us.

ROMANS 8:35,37

Those things we consider difficulties are often
God's opportunities for our greater blessing.
We must trust, believe, hope, and continue to
walk the path he has laid before us.

May our Lord Jesus Christ himself and God our
Father, who loved us and by his grace gave us
eternal encouragement and good hope, encourage
your hearts and strengthen you in every good deed
and word.

2 THESSALONIANS 2:16—17

God Is With Us...
In Our
Confusion

I just don't understand
why, when I needed You
most, You leave me.

Many things in life cannot be explained: the death of an infant, the loss of a job, the rebellion of a child, the desertion by a loved one, or any number of other circumstances beyond our control. Have you ever wondered, Why did this have to happen? God can help us with those "Why?" questions.

[David questioned God,] "Has his unfailing love vanished forever? Has his promise failed for all time? Has God forgotten to be merciful? Has he in anger withheld his compassion?"

PSALM 77:8—9

"My thoughts are not your thoughts, neither are your ways my ways," declares the Lord. "As the heavens are higher than the earth, so are my ways higher than your ways and my thoughts than your thoughts."

ISAIAH 55:8—9

When faced with bewildering circumstances, we are tempted to ask "Why?" But a better question to ask is "What?…What do you have in mind now, Lord?"

> "Call to me and I will answer you and tell you great and unsearchable things you do not know," [says the Lord.]
>
> JEREMIAH 33:3

> Cast your cares on the Lord and he will sustain you; he will never let the righteous fall.
>
> PSALM 55:22

> Let us acknowledge the Lord; let us press on to acknowledge him. As surely as the sun rises, he will appear; he will come to us like the winter rains, like the spring rains that water the earth.
>
> HOSEA 6:3

> [O Lord,] it was good for me to be afflicted so that I might learn your decrees.
>
> PSALM 119:71

Though it may sometimes seem that things are out of control, we can take comfort in God's enduring promises and constant presence.

[The Lord says,] "Do not fear, for I am with you; do not be dismayed, for I am your God. I will strengthen you and help you; I will uphold you with my righteous right hand."

ISAIAH 41:10

A righteous man may have many troubles, but the Lord delivers him from them all.

PSALM 34:19

"I will make an everlasting covenant with them: I will never stop doing good to them," [says the Lord.]

JEREMIAH 32:40

Your love, O Lord, endures forever.

PSALM 138:8

Be strong and courageous. Do not be terrified; do not be discouraged, for the Lord your God will be with you wherever you go.

JOSHUA 1:9

Let us hold unswervingly to the hope we profess,
for [God] who promised is faithful.

HEBREWS 10:23

God, who has called you into fellowship with his
Son Jesus Christ our Lord, is faithful.

1 CORINTHIANS 1:9

Who is a God like you, who pardons sin and
forgives the transgression of the remnant of his
inheritance? You do not stay angry forever
but delight to show mercy. You will again have
compassion on us.

MICAH 7:18–19

His mercy extends to those who fear him,
from generation to generation.

LUKE 1:50

This I call to mind and therefore I have hope:
Because of the Lord's great love we are not consumed, for his compassions never fail. They are
new every morning; great is your faithfulness.

LAMENTATIONS 3:21–23

Commit to the Lord whatever you do, and your plans will succeed.

PROVERBS 16:3

The Lord is good to those whose hope is in him, to the one who seeks him.

LAMENTATIONS 3:25

[O Lord,] you are my hiding place; you will protect me from trouble and surround me with songs of deliverance.

PSALM 32:7

Blessed are you who hunger now, for you will be satisfied. Blessed are you who weep now, for you will laugh.

LUKE 6:21

Put away all doubts. Cast out all confusion. Stand firm in the work of the Lord, and find a renewed faith following in his footsteps.

The Lord is my strength and my shield; my heart trusts in him, and I am helped. My heart leaps for joy and I will give thanks to him.

PSALM 28:7

God Is With Us...
As Our
Loving Father

He whispered, "My precious child..."

The Creator of the universe calls me his child—what a blessing! What a privilege! What a responsibility!

> The Lord disciplines those he loves, as a father the son he delights in.
>
> PROVERBS 3:12

> "I will be a Father to you, and you will be my sons and daughters, says the Lord Almighty."
>
> 2 CORINTHIANS 6:18

> Endure hardship as discipline; God is treating you as sons. For what son is not disciplined by his father?
>
> HEBREWS 12:7

> [David declared,] "You are my Father, my God, the Rock my Savior."
>
> PSALM 89:26

> To us a child is born, to us a son is given, and the government will be on his shoulders. And he will be called... Everlasting Father.
>
> ISAIAH 9:6

O Lord, you are our Father. We are the clay, you are the potter; we are all the work of your hand.

ISAIAH 64:8

You did not receive a spirit that makes you a slave again to fear, but you received the Spirit of sonship. And by him we cry, "Abba, Father."

ROMANS 8:15

For us there is but one God, the Father, from whom all things came and for whom we live; and there is but one Lord, Jesus Christ, through whom all things came and through whom we live.

1 CORINTHIANS 8:6

There is one body and one Spirit—just as you were called to one hope when you were called—one Lord, one faith, one baptism; one God and Father of all, who is over all and through all and in all.

EPHESIANS 4:4–6

How great is the love the Father has lavished on us, that we should be called children of God!

1 JOHN 3:1

You, O Lord, are our Father, our Redeemer from of old is your name.

ISAIAH 63:16

As children of God we can trust that our
Father will provide for us.

> Your Father knows what you need before you
> ask him.
>
> MATTHEW 6:8

> Which of you fathers, if your son asks for a fish,
> will give him a snake instead? Or if he asks for an
> egg, will give him a scorpion? If you then, though
> you are evil, know how to give good gifts to your
> children, how much more will your Father in
> heaven give the Holy Spirit to those who ask him!
>
> LUKE 11:11–13

As God's children, our Father knows us
by name and bestows on us certain rights,
privileges, and responsibilities.

> I, the Lord, have called you in righteousness;
> I will take hold of your hand. I will keep you
> and will make you to be a covenant for the people
> and a light for the Gentiles.
>
> ISAIAH 42:6

This is what the Lord says ... he who formed you... "Fear not, for I have redeemed you; I have summoned you by name; you are mine."

ISAIAH 43:1

"I will pour out my Spirit on your offspring, and my blessing on your descendants. They will spring up like grass in a meadow, like poplar trees by flowing streams. One will say, 'I belong to the Lord'; another will call himself by the name of Jacob; still another will write on his hand, 'The Lord's.' "

ISAIAH 44:3–5

Before I was born the Lord called me; from my birth he has made mention of my name.

ISAIAH 49:1

Our loving Father cares for us as a shepherd cares for his sheep. And we, his children, need to listen carefully to his voice and obey.

The sheep listen to his voice. He calls his own sheep by name and leads them out. When he has brought out all his own, he goes on ahead of them, and his sheep follow him because they know his voice.

JOHN 10:3–4

[Jesus said,] "I am the good shepherd; I know my sheep and my sheep know me—just as the Father knows me and I know the Father—and I lay down my life for the sheep."

JOHN 10:14–15

[Jesus said,] "My sheep listen to my voice; I know them, and they follow me."

JOHN 10:27

God Is With Us...
Always!

"...I love you and will never leave you, never, ever, during your trials and testings."

We often make promises we can't keep. God isn't like that. God is faithful and trustworthy. When God promises never to leave us, he means just what he says. He's not going anywhere!

God has said, "Never will I leave you; never will I forsake you."

HEBREWS 13:5

The Lord himself goes before you and will be with you; he will never leave you nor forsake you. Do not be afraid; do not be discouraged.

DEUTERONOMY 31:8

"No one will be able to stand up against you all the days of your life. As I was with Moses, so I will be with you; I will never leave you nor forsake you," [says the Lord.]

JOSHUA 1:5

[Jesus replied,] "Surely I am with you always, to the very end of the age."

MATTHEW 28:20

Do not fear, for I am with you; do not be dismayed, for I am your God. I will strengthen you and help you; I will uphold you with my righteous right hand.

ISAIAH 41:10

I am convinced that neither death nor life, neither angels nor demons, neither the present nor the future, nor any powers, neither height nor depth, nor anything else in all creation, will be able to separate us from the love of God that is in Christ Jesus our Lord.

ROMANS 8:38–39

"Though the mountains be shaken and the hills be removed, yet my unfailing love for you will not be shaken nor my covenant of peace be removed," says the Lord, who has compassion on you.

ISAIAH 54:10

"Here I am! I stand at the door and knock. If anyone hears my voice and opens the door, I will come in and eat with him, and he with me," [says the Lord.]

REVELATION 3:20

"He will call upon me, and I will answer him;
I will be with him in trouble," [says the Lord.]

PSALM 91:15

Be strong and courageous. Do not be terrified;
do not be discouraged, for the Lord your God
will be with you wherever you go.

JOSHUA 1:9

The Lord watches over you— the Lord is your shade
at your right hand; the sun will not harm you by
day, nor the moon by night. The Lord will keep
you from all harm— he will watch over your life;
the Lord will watch over your coming and going
both now and forevermore.

PSALM 121:5–8

When it seems that life is whirling out of control, we can take comfort in God's sovereignty and power. He has everything under control. And he will work his will in every circumstance.

Commit your way to the Lord; trust in him and he will do this: He will make your righteousness shine like the dawn, the justice of your cause like the noonday sun.

PSALM 37:5–6

Commit to the Lord whatever you do, and your plans will succeed.

PROVERBS 16:3

Do not be anxious about anything, but in everything, by prayer and petition, with thanksgiving, present your requests to God. And the peace of God, which transcends all understanding, will guard your hearts and your minds in Christ Jesus.

PHILIPPIANS 4:6–7

Many are the plans in a man's heart, but it is the Lord's purpose that prevails.

PROVERBS 19:21

The Lord Almighty has purposed, and who can thwart him? His hand is stretched out, and who can turn it back?

ISAIAH 14:27

"I make known the end from the beginning, from ancient times, what is still to come. I say: My purpose will stand, and I will do all that I please," [says the Lord.]

ISAIAH 46:10

Look at the birds of the air; they do not sow or reap or store away in barns, and yet your heavenly Father feeds them. Are you not much more valuable than they? Who of you by worrying can add a single hour to his life?

MATTHEW 6:26—27

I know that you can do all things; no plan of yours can be thwarted, [O Lord.]

JOB 42:2

I know that everything God does will endure forever; nothing can be added to it and nothing taken from it. God does it so that men will revere him.

ECCLESIASTES 3:14

The Lord gives strength to his people; the Lord blesses his people with peace.

PSALM 29:11

My flesh and my heart may fail, but God is the strength of my heart and my portion forever.

PSALM 73:26

[O Lord,] great peace have they who love your law, and nothing can make them stumble.

PSALM 119:165

Those who trust in the Lord are like Mount Zion, which cannot be shaken but endures forever.

PSALM 125:1

Whenever we hit rock-bottom, we can be assured of God's love and care. His encouragement breathes new possibilities into impossible circumstances.

Let us then approach the throne of grace with confidence, so that we may receive mercy and find grace to help us in our time of need.

HEBREWS 4:16

In you, O Lord, I have taken refuge; let me never be put to shame; deliver me in your righteousness.

PSALM 31:1

The Lord is with me; I will not be afraid.

PSALM 118:6

Taste and see that the Lord is good; blessed is the man who takes refuge in him.

PSALM 34:8

So we say with confidence, "The Lord is my helper; I will not be afraid. What can man do to me?"

HEBREWS 13:6

God Is With Us...
As Our
Strong Provider

"When you saw only one
set of footprints, it was
then that I carried you."

Our problems may seem overwhelming, but God's power is stronger than any obstacle we may face.

I am the Lord, the God of all mankind. Is anything too hard for me?

All that we have accomplished you have done for us, [O Lord.]

ISAIAH 26:12

[God] does as he pleases with the powers of heaven and the peoples of the earth. No one can hold back his hand or say to him: "What have you done?"

DANIEL 4:35

You are the ruler of all things. In your hands are strength and power to exalt and give strength to all. Now, our God, we give you thanks, and praise your glorious name.

1 CHRONICLES 29:12–13

With God all things are possible.

MATTHEW 19:26

The Lord is slow to anger and great in power...
His way is in the whirlwind and the storm, and
clouds are the dust of his feet.

NAHUM 1:3

I can do everything through Christ who gives
me strength.

PHILIPPIANS 4:13

Be strong in the Lord and in his mighty power.

EPHESIANS 6:10

The eternal God is your refuge, and underneath
are the everlasting arms.

DEUTERONOMY 33:27

The Lord gives strength to his people; the Lord
blesses his people with peace.

PSALM 29:11

[The Lord] said to me, "My grace is sufficient for
you, for my power is made perfect in weakness."

2 CORINTHIANS 12:9

The Lord is the strength of his people, a fortress
of salvation for his anointed one.

PSALM 28:8

In the Lord alone are righteousness and strength.

ISAIAH 45:24

"I will strengthen them in the Lord and in his
name they will walk," declares the Lord.

ZECHARIAH 10:12

"I will refresh the weary and satisfy the faint,"
[says the Lord.]

JEREMIAH 31:25

Since God is our strong Provider, we can be
assured that he is in control of every aspect
of our lives. He will prepare the way before
us. He will never leave us. And he will provide
our every need.

Those who know your name will trust in you,
for you, Lord, have never forsaken those who
seek you.

PSALM 9:10

[Jesus taught his disciples saying,] "If you believe,
you will receive whatever you ask for in prayer."

MATTHEW 21:22

No eye has seen, no ear has heard, no mind has
conceived what God has prepared for those who
love him.

1 CORINTHIANS 2:9

My God will meet all your needs according to his
glorious riches in Christ Jesus.

PHILIPPIANS 4:19

[Jesus said,] "Come to me, all you who are weary
and burdened, and I will give you rest."

MATTHEW 11:28

"Before they call I will answer; while they are still
speaking I will hear," [declares the Lord.]

ISAIAH 65:24

Taste and see that the Lord is good; blessed is the man who takes refuge in him.

PSALM 34:8

O Lord Almighty, blessed is the man who trusts in you.

PSALM 84:12

Those who trust in the Lord are like Mount Zion, which cannot be shaken but endures forever.

PSALM 125:1

He who did not spare his own Son, but gave him up for us all—how will he not also, along with him, graciously give us all things?

ROMANS 8:32

Praise the Lord, O my soul, and forget not all his benefits— who forgives all your sins and heals all your diseases, who redeems your life from the pit and crowns you with love and compassion, who satisfies your desires with good things so that your youth is renewed like the eagle's.

PSALM 103:2—5

Praise be to the Lord, to God our Savior,
who daily bears our burdens.

PSALM 68:19

You will keep in perfect peace him whose mind
is steadfast, because he trusts in you, [O Lord.]

ISAIAH 26:3

The Lord longs to be gracious to you; he rises
to show you compassion. For the Lord is a God
of justice. Blessed are all who wait for him!

ISAIAH 30:18

Trust in the Lord with all your heart and lean
not on your own understanding.

PROVERBS 3:5

He who trusts in the Lord will prosper.

PROVERBS 28:25

As the Scripture says, "Anyone who trusts
in [Christ] will never be put to shame."

ROMANS 10:11

Our God is strong enough to carry us,
but also gentle enough to enfold us in his
loving embrace.

[God] tends his flock like a shepherd: He gathers
the lambs in his arms and carries them close to his
heart; he gently leads those that have young.

ISAIAH 40:11

[The Lord] makes me lie down in green pastures,
he leads me beside quiet waters, he restores my
soul. He guides me in paths of righteousness for
his name's sake.

PSALM 23:2–3

[Jesus taught them saying,] "Come to me, all you
who are weary and burdened, and I will give you
rest. Take my yoke upon you and learn from me,
for I am gentle and humble in heart, and you will
find rest for your souls. For my yoke is easy and my
burden is light."

MATTHEW 11:28–30

As our strong Provider carries us over the rough places in our lives, he speaks words of peace and blessing to our wounded hearts.

The Lord bless you and keep you; the Lord make his face shine upon you and be gracious to you; the Lord turn his face toward you and give you peace.

NUMBERS 6:24–26

May the God of peace…equip you with everything good for doing his will, and may he work in us what is pleasing to him, through Jesus Christ, to whom be glory for ever and ever. Amen.

HEBREWS 13:20–21

If you have enjoyed this book,
Hallmark would love
to hear from you.

Please send comments to:
Book Feedback
2501 McGee, Mail Drop 215
Kansas City, MO 64141-6580
Or e-mail us at:
booknotes@hallmark.com